D
Dl

A selection of words and anecdotes
from around Dorset

by
Gill Newton

BRADWELL
BOOKS

Published by Bradwell Books
9 Orgreave Close Sheffield S13 9NP
Email: books@bradwellbooks.co.uk

British Library Cataloguing in Publication Data:
a catalogue record for this book is available from
the British Library.

1st Edition

ISBN: 9781910551011

Design and artwork by: Andrew Caffrey

Print: Gomer Press, Llandysul, Ceredigion SA44 4JL

Image Credits: iStock, Creative Commons
& pastandpresentpublications.com

Introduction

It was the *Piddles* and the *Puddles* which first brought the vivid language of Dorset to life for me. During childhood visits to the county, I was told about the fascinating history behind Dorset place names such as *Piddletrenthide* and *Tolpuddle!* Those names were my first insight into the words associated with the area, many of which have great character while others, as we see in this book, have a more risqué meaning in modern times!

Many of us naturally think of THOMAS HARDY when it comes to considering the association between Dorset and words. While there's no doubt, as we will see briefly in this book, that Hardy's contribution is extensive and inspiring, many other writers have had a connection with Dorset too. With a particular view on dialect, it is WILLIAM BARNES we have to thank for capturing so much of the county's language. His poems and glossary have been instrumental in keeping the language of Dorset's past alive. Yet, as we see in this book, while Barnes's works are acknowledged to be of great importance, there are some who feel that he is still undervalued outside of Dorset.

Take a close look at the glossary in the first part of the book to discover just how poetic the Dorset dialect is, from

the wonderful word *'dumbledore'* to *'goocoo'* to *'joppety-joppety'*!
Then explore the sayings which were once commonplace
in the county. You'll find out why you wouldn't want to be
called a *'Lawrence'* or a *'lablolly'* and why to *'goo snacks'* does
not mean heading off the local shop for a sandwich! Even
the local food holds hints of the area's fascinating past,
as with the names *Blue Vinny Cheese* and *Piddle Bacon Cake*
(back to those *Piddles* and *Puddles* again!). While we're on
the topic of food, read on to find out why people in Dorset
love throwing their food around and why we have Dorset to
thank for one of our most well-known vegetables!

West Country accents have often been unfairly associated
with comedy. Yet the folk singers of the county have always
relished the potential for humour in their dialect. As we see
in this book, bands like THE YETTIES have helped to bring
the dialect to greater public recognition. Reading Dorset
dialect is one thing. Hearing it is something else. It's
incredible to be able to listen to it through the wonderful
recordings of conversations, folk songs and more on the
British Library website. But let's not look at Dorset dialect
as a thing of the past. Even Dorset's motto is in the local
dialect! Words still have great power in the county, as you'll
discover when you read why you must never give *'underground
mutton'* its proper name if you're ever in Portland!

4

It's all too easy to have a perception of a place and its dialect based on just a few aspects. Yet, like most places, the closer you look, the more there is to Dorset and its language. There's no denying that Dorset is indeed a rural place with a rich agricultural past. But scratch away at the surface (and sadly we can only do this briefly here in this book) and you'll discover a county which truly lives up to its motto. Where else would you find a place which is as significant for swans, as it is for its role in the beginnings of the trade union movement and of *Trivial Pursuit*?

Happy exploring!

Weymouth Beach People Past & Present Publications

List of some Dorset words with a few hints on Dorset word-shapes

THE MAIN SOUNDS:

1. *ee in beet.*

2. *e in Dorset* (a sound between 1 and 3.)

3. *a in mate.*

4. *i in birth.*

5. *a in father.*

6. *aw in awe.*

7. *o in dote.*

8. *oo in rood.*

In Dorset words which are forms of book-English ones, the Dorset words differ from the others mainly by Grimm's law, that 'likes shift into likes', and I have given a few hints by which the putting of an English heading for the Dorset one will give the English word. If the reader is posed by dreaten, he may try for dr, thr, which will bring out threaten.

From *Poems of Rural Life in the Dorset Dialect*,
by WILLIAM BARNES

Glossary

A

Aggy – to gather eggs

Ailen – an illness

Anigh – near to

Ankly – ankle

Any-when – at any time

Archet – orchard

Amary Cheese – cheese made out of skimmed milk

A-strout – stretched

Avore – before

Avroze – frozen

Ax – to ask

Axen – ashes

Ayer – air

B

Backhouse – outhouse

Backside – the back yard of a house

Bait – to restore or refresh

Ballyrag – to scold

Bandy – a long heavy stick with a bent end, used to move dung in the fields

Barken – barley or barley straw

Barry – to borrow

Batch – hillock

Battenbuoard – a thatcher's tool for beating down thatch

Baven – a faggot made of long untrimmed wood

Beass – cattle

Beat-plough – a turfcutting tool

Beens – because

Bee-pot – bee-hive

Beetle or **Bwitle** – a large mallet for driving wedges

Beetlehead – bullhead or miller's thumb

Bennits – the stems of the bent grass

Biddle – beetle

Bide – dwell or live

Bimeby – by-and-by, soon

Birdkipper – a person who was employed to keep birds away from corn

Bit an' drap – a bit of food and a drop of drink

Bit an' crimp – Every bit an' crumb. Every little bit of something

Biver – to shake or quiver as with cold or fear

Blatch – black or soot

Blather – an uproar

Blooth or **Blowth** – the blossom of fruit trees

Bottom – steadfastness

Bremble – bramble

Brinten – bold, impudent, audacious

Brockle – to break

Bruckly – brittle

Budget – a leather pouch in which a mower carried his whetstone

Bumbye – by-and-by

C

Caddie – confusion, uproar

Caddle – muddle

Car – to carry: to car hay is to stack hay

Carner-cubord – a right-angled cupboard to fit the comer of a room

Cazelty weather – casualty weather, i.e. stormy

Chammer – chamber, bedroom

Chaw – to chew

Cheese-late or **Cheese-lote** – a cheese loft or floor to dry cheese on

Chimley – chimney

Chop – to sell or deal; to barter or exchange

Chump – a log of wood

Cider-wring – cider press

Clacker or **Bird-clacker** – a type kind of rattle to frighten away birds from a cornfield

Clavy – mantelpiece

Clinker – icicle

Clock – a once common ornament on the ankles of stockings

Cockle – to tangle

Cowheart – a coward

Cowlease – an unmown field

Cradlehood – infancy

Cricket – a low stool for a child

Criss-cross-lain – the alphabet

Crousty – ill-tempered

Crowd – a fiddle

Culver – a wood pigeon, a dove

Curdle – curl (hair)

Cute, acute – sharp, cunning

D

Dabster – an expert

Dadder – to bewilder

Daes – days

Dander – anger

Dewbit – the first meal in the morning, not as substantial as a regular breakfast

Didden – did not

Dockspitter – a tool for pulling or cutting up docks

Dogs – iron utensils which used to stand at the sides of the hearth to keep up the sticks of a wood fire

Doughbiaked – of weak or inactive mind

Dousty – dusty

Dout – extinguish

Downdaishous – audacious

Drashel – threshold

Drawlatcheten – lazy

Drinky – intoxicated

Duckish – dull, dark

Drong or **Drongway** – to compress. A narrow way between two hedges or walls

Dumbledore, Durable or **Dummel** – dull or a bumblebee

Dunch-pudden – hard or plain pudding made of only flour and water

E

Eale – ale

Eesterdae – yesterday

Eet – yet

Effets – newts

Emmets – ants

Emmet-butt or **Emmet-hill** – anthill

Evemen – evening

F

Faddle – a pack or bundle

Fantod – a fuss

Fess – proud

Figgety-pudden – plum pudding

Flummocks – to frighten

Footling – beneath contempt

Footy – little, insignificant

Frith – brushwood

Furmenty – frumenty (spiced porridge made from hulled wheat)

G

Gake or **Gawk** – a cuckoo; to go or stand and stare about idly like a cuckoo

Gally-crow – scarecrow

Gammon – to play sport with another

Gannywedge – to yawn, to open, to spread

Gee, jee – to agree, to go on well together

Gifts – white spots on the fingernails, believed to be a sign of coming presents! *'Gifts on the thumb sure to come; Gifts on the finger sure to linger.'*

Gilcup, Giltcup or **Giltycup** – buttercup

Girt – great

Glene – to joke or jest

Glow – to stare, to watch with fixed and wide-open eyes

Glutch – to swallow

Goocoo – cuckoo

Gramfer – Grandfather

Grammer – Grandmother

Greygole – bluebell

Gumption – sense, wit

Gurgens – pollard, coarse flour

Gwain – going

Gwains-on – riotous behaviour

H

Hacker – a hoe

Halterpath – a road for people on horseback, but not for carriages

Handy – approximate

Han'pat – fit or ready at hand

Hard-worken – industrious

Harvest-man – the cranefly or daddy-long-legs

Hatch – a wicket or little gate

Heal – to cover

Hedlen – headlong

Hethcropper – a horse bred on a heath

Hidy-buck – a game of hide and seek

Hike off or out – to hasten, to rush

Ho – to he careful or anxious

Hold wi' – agree with

Homhle – a duck

Honey-zuck – the honeysuckle

Hoss-stinger – the dragon fly

I

Ice-candle – an icicle

Inon – an onion

J

Janders – jaundice

Jist, Jis' – just

Joppety-joppety – nervous trepidation

K

Keech – to cut grass and weeds on the side of rivers

Kiale-leaf and **Kiale-stump** – a cabbage leaf or cabbage stump

Kit – acquaintance or kindred

Kitty boots – a kind of laced-up boots which reached up over the ankles

L

Lamploo – an outdoor game that boys used to play

Lavish – rank

Leery – hungry

Lerret – large boat

Lew – sheltered

Limber – slender

Limner – a painter

Lip – a basket or chest

Lippen or **Lippy** – wet, rainy

Lisome – cheerful

Litter – confusion

Lote or **Late** – a loft

Lowsen – to listen

M

Magot – a whim or fancy, an experiment

Main – strength, might

Mampus – a great number, a crowd

Mel – to meddle

Mesh – moss

Mid be – may be

Min – a word of contempt

Mistructful – suspicious

Moud – a field mouse

N

Nammet – noon meat, luncheon
Naps, Knee-naps – leathers worn over the knees by thatchers at work
Near – stingy, miserly
Nicky – very small short-cut bundles of wood for lighting coal fires
Nippy – hungry
Nirrup – donkey
Not – a flower bed or plot
Nunch or **Nunchen** – from noon. The noon meal or luncheon

O

Outdoor work – field work
Out ov ban' – immediately, without delay
Overright – opposite
Oves hook – a thatcher's hook for trimming the eaves

P

Parrick – a paddock, a small enclosed field

Peart – well, lively

Peck upon – to domineer

Pelt – a wave of anger

Piaviours – paving stones, flag stones

Pirty – pretty

Pitty deal – a great deal

Pleace – place

Popples or **Popplestuones** – pebbles

Prog – food

Pure – quite well

Q

Quickzet hedge – a planted living hedge in distinction from a dead fence

Quine – the comer of a wall

Quob – to quiver

R

Rag – to scold, to accuse with bitter words

Rale – to walk

Ramshacklum – good for nothing

Rap – to barter, to exchange articles

Rate – to scold

Rathe – early

Rean – to eat up greedily

Reaphook – a sickle

Reddick – robin

Reeve – to unravel

Reremouse – a hat

Rottletraps – rickety old household goods

Dorchester Cornhill Past & Present Publications

S

Saassy or **Sassy** – saucy

Satepoll – a silly person

Scaly – stingy

Scram – small, awkward

Sives – Chive, garlic

Sliee – a broad short-handled firepan for wood fires
Smitch – a cloud of dust
Snabble – to eat up hastily or greedily
Solid – solid, also serious or gentle
Span-new – wholly clean or new
Spik – Lavender
Sprack – lively, active
Spry – Lively
Stick – a colloquial name for a tree
Stud – mystified

T

Tack – a shelf
Tallet – a hayloft over a stable
Tarble, Tarblish – tolerable, pretty well
Tiaken – attractive, winning, captivating
Tilty – irritable, hot tempered
Tinklebobs – icicles
Torrididdle – bewildered, distracted
T'other and **T'otherum** – the other and the others.
To-year – this year; used like today, tonight, tomorrow
Trig – sound and firm
Turmit – turnip
Tuoad's meat – toadstool
Twanketen – melancholy

U

Undercreepen – sly, hypocritical
Underhan' – not fair and open
Up-on-end – perpendicular
Upseedown, Upsidown – overturned

V

Vang – to earn
Vess – a verse; to vessy is to read verses in turn
Viaries' fiazen or **Viaries' hearts** – Fossils common in
the chalk and gravel formations of Dorset once believed
to be the heads or hearts of fairies
Viaryring – a fairy ring
Vinny or **Vinnied** – mouldy: Blue Vinny or vinnied cheese
is a famous Dorset cheese
Vitty – Properly, neatly

W

Wayzalt – a children's game in which two, locking their
arms in each other back to back, alternately lift each
other from the ground
Weir or **Ware** – a pond
Welshnut – a walnut

Werret – to worry

Wont – a mole

Wonthill – a molehill

Woodquest – a woodpigeon

Woppen – big, weighty

Wopsy – wasp

Wordle – world

Y

Yt – you

Yakker – an acorn

Yal – ale

Yis – earthworm

Yop – to talk rapidly

Z

Za – to saw

Zeale – sack

Zet up – to make very angry

Zich – such

Zilt – to salt

Zive – a scythe

Zummat – something

Zwail – to swagger

Swanage Past & Present Publications

Old Dorset Sayings

'Zet the fox to keep the geese' – A proverb used to describe a person who had unwisely put their trust in someone who was likely to let them down.

'Don't ye teach your grammer to spin' – As you'll have guessed, this is a more rural version of the classic saying *'Don't teach your grandmother to suck eggs'*; i.e. don't try to give instructions to someone who already knows better than you!

'All the goo' – All the fashion!

'Good-now' – This phrase meant about the same as *'Do you know'* or *'You must know'*.

'Niver'fitide' – This was a great word which was used in the following type of context: *'That'll be next niver'stide'*, meaning that it will never happen!

'Larrence' or *'Lawrence'* – This was an interesting quirk of the dialect that Barnes explained in one of his books as follows:

> *From some cause which the author has not yet found, Lawrence is in some parts of Dorset the patron or personification of laziness. Whien one is seen to be lazy Lawrence is said to have him ; and when one feels a loathing of exertion he sometimes cries : 'Liazy Larrence let me goo, Don't hold me zummer an winter too.'*

'Imma'bbee' – It may be.

'Not to hitch oones bosses together' – This proverb, which has a distinctly rural feel, describes when two people do not agree with one another.

'To hold wi' the hiare an run wi' the houns' – This saying is essentially about someone who is trying to cover all bases, showing that they are friends with someone and yet being on the side of their enemies!

'*Snacks*' or rather '*To goo snacks*' – This phrase means to be partners and to share the gains of a project or initiative.

'*I da live too near a wood to be frightened by an owl*' – This is a lovely expression which means '*I understand matters too well*' or I know too much of such things to be frightened.'

'*To*' – this was used in Dorset with '*where*': '*Where d'ye bide to?*' '*Where is it to?*'

'*Took to*' – A person is described as being '*a-took to*' when they have met someone who is a match for them.

'*Shark*' or '*Shark off*' – to sneak off softly from shame or due to a sense of coming danger.

'*Tea with a dash of rum is called 'milk from the brown cow*'; the dead are '*put to bed with a shovel*'; a noisy old man is a '*blaze wig*'; a fat and pompous fellow is a '*blow-poke*'; the thoughts of the flighty girl go *a-'bell-wavering*'; the gallows is the '*black horse foaled by an acorn.*' The Dorset rustic has devised many names for the dullard: '*billy-buttons,*' '*billy-whiffler,*' '*lablolly,*' '*ninnyhammer,*' and '*bluffle-head*' are some of them. The very sound of such names suggests folly.

'Leer' is a curious word still heard in Dorset and Devon. It is used to express the sense of craving produced by weakness and long fasting. Perhaps Shakespeare used Lear in a metaphorical sense. I remember once hearing a Sussex labourer speak of taking his

'coager' (cold cheer?), a meal of cold victuals taken at noon, but I am told the mouthful of bread and cheese taken at starting in the morning by the Dorset rustic rejoices in the still more delightful name of 'dew-bit'.

From *Thomas Hardy's Dorset* by ROBERT THURSTON HOPKINS, *published 1922*

Where did Dorset get its name?

Dorset is an old name which originally comes from the name of Dorchester, its county town. Dorchester was where the Romans set up a settlement right back in the first century AD, calling it Durnovaria. Durnovaria is the Latin version of an Old Brittonic word which was believed to mean *'place with fist-sized pebbles'*! It was the Saxons who went on to call the place Dornwaraceaster (ceaster was the Old English name for a Roman town). The name Dornsæte then started being used as the name for the inhabitants of the area. This was from 'Dorn', which is a shortened version of Dornwaraceaster, and the Old English word sæte, which means 'people'. The first time it was called this was in AD 845 in the Anglo-Saxon Chronicle. But it wasn't until the 10th century that the county's name, 'Dorseteschyre' (Dorsetshire), was first recorded.

Dorsetshire – in the Sason Chronicles Dorstxta, in Domesday Dortete – takes its name from the original inhabitants, the Dorsaetas; who, in turn, derive their appellation in its Latinized form of Durotrices, waterside dwellers, from the two British words, Dwr = water, and trigo, to dwell; probably because the headquarters of the tribe were by the side of some inlet or piece of water; perhaps the Poole inlet, running up to Wareham.

'The chief resources of Dorsetshire are agricultural. The dairy produce is large ; and there is a great deal of corn grown. About Bridport hemp is much cultivated, to supply the rope and twine works of that town, there are silk-throwing mills at Sherborne, and elsewhere. The ship and yacht builders of Poole are favourably known. Poole is the chief port of the county. Its trade is almost entirely coasting. The quarries of Purbeck and Portland are of great

celebrity for their excellent building stone. There is a very extensive manufacture of pottery and tiles in the vicinity of Wareham and Poole, and potters'-clay and pipe-clay are lately dug, and exported from the same district.

From *Handbook for Travellers in Wiltshire, Dorsetshire and Somersetshire* by JOHN MURRAY, *published in 1869*

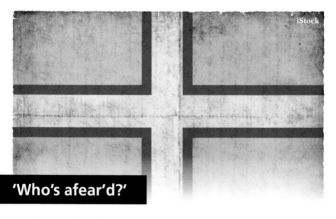

'Who's afear'd?'

'*Who's afear'd*' is the bold motto of Dorset. It was one of four originally suggested, including LORD SHAFTESBURY's idea: '*Excellence where Beauty Reigns*'. '*Who's afear'd?*' was adopted by the Society of Dorset Men in 1905 at the suggestion of THOMAS HARDY. It was converted to Dorset dialect by them in 1908, and then suggested to the County Council by a COLONEL C.D. DREW, who was the curator of the Dorset County Museum.

William Barnes: a Dorset dialect hero

One name above all others is closely associated with preserving and promoting the dialect of Dorset. But how did a schoolteacher go on to write more than 800 poems, become synonymous with the dialect of his region and end up being a tutor to THOMAS HARDY? WILLIAM BARNES was born the son of a farmer in Bagber in 1801. He quickly went on to an illustrious academic career which included a role as a Church of England minister, and started contributing his Dorset dialect poems to periodicals. As well as producing collections of poems, *Poems of Rural Life in the Dorset Dialect*, *Hwomely Rhymes* and a third

William Barnes Creative Commons

collection in 1863, Barnes also wrote grammatical books and a *Glossary of Dorset Dialect (1863)*. His comprehensive English grammar quotes from no fewer than 70 languages! Barnes was apparently very much against the corruption of the English language with Greek and Roman terms.

Admired by the greats

Barnes earned the admiration of his fellow Victorian poets and is thought to have been a significant influence on both Hardy and Hopkins. On his death, Hardy wrote the poem *'The Last Signal'* for him. *'My Orcha'd in Linden Lea'* – one of Barnes's poems – was later set to music by RALPH VAUGHAN WILLIAMS. Barnes's legacy is kept alive to this day in the Barnes Collection at the Dorset History Centre in Dorchester.

Pronunciation guide

While Barnes is recognised for his legacy, there are some who believe that he deserves greater acclaim for his role in promoting and preserving Dorset's dialect. One of these people is THOMAS BURTON, Associate Professor of English from the University of Adelaide. In order to help make Barnes's work accessible to others, Burton recently completed a pronunciation guide for *Poems of Rural Life in the Dorset Dialect* (source: BBC).

'England's Rabbie Burns'

Many believe that Barnes's value is still underestimated, with one journalist describing him as *'England's Rabbie Burns'* because of his drive to capture the voice and the reality of the working man and woman.

But what was it that made Barnes love the Dorset dialect so much? It was thought that, in his view, the dialect was a purer version of English than anywhere else because it did not feature any Latin or French words. Barnes also valued the fact that the dialect was enriched by the language of the working man and woman. Read on to discover some of Barnes's poems for yourself.

> *William Barnes, the Dorset poet, enumerates the chief peculiarities of the Dorset dialect in his books on speech lore. He loved the odd phrases of children, and it is easy to see why. For a child, not knowing the correct method of describing a thing and seeking to express its meaning, will often go back to the strong old Anglo-Saxon definitions. The child can often coin very apt phrases. As, for instance, the Dorset child who spoke of honey as 'bee-jam'. Barnes was delighted, too, with the boy 'who scrope out the "p" in "psalm" 'cose it didn't spell nothen'.*

He always has that deep, quiet craving for the hearth, the fire, the protecting thatch of a cottage, which gives his work a pathetic touch. I think sometimes that Barnes must have been nearer to being cold, homeless and tired at times than is generally understood.

From *Thomas Hardy's Dorset* by ROBERT THURSTON HOPKINS

There is no doubt that he is the best pastoral poet we possess, the most sincere, the most genuine, the most theocritan; and that the dialect is but a very thin veil hiding from us some of the most delicate and finished verse written in our time.

Obituary of
WILLIAM BARNES
in *The Saturday Review*

The Grave of William Barnes
Creative Commons

Poems by William Barnes

From *Poems in the Dorset Dialect* by WILLIAM BARNES,
published 1864

Praise o' Dorset

We Do'set, though we mid be hwomely,
Be'nt asheam'd to own our pleace;
An' we've zome women not uncomely,
Nor asheam'd to show their feace ;
We've a mead or two wo'th mowen,
We've an ox or two wo'th showen,
In the village.
At the tillage,
Come along an' you shall vind
That Do'set men don't sheame their kind,
Friend an' wife,
Faethers, mothers, sisters, brothers,
Happy, happy, be their life!
Vor Do'set dear,
Then gi'e oone cheer;
D'ye hear? Oone cheer !

An' if in Do'set you be roamen,
An' ha' bus'ness at a farm,
Then woont ye zee your eale a-foamen,
Or your cider down to warm?
Woont ye have brown bread a-put ye,

An' some vinny cheese a-cut ye?
Butter? Rolls o't!
Cream? Whyiowls o't!
Woont ye have, in short, your vill,
A-gi'ed wi' a right good will?
Friend an' wife,
Faethers, mothers, sisters, brothers,
Happy, happy, be their life!
Vor Do'set dear,
Then gi'e oone cheer;
D'ye hear? Oone cheer I

An woont ye have vor ev'ry shillen,
Shillen's wo'th at any shop,
Though Do'set chaps l'e up to zellen,
An' can meake a tidy swop?
Use em well, they'll use you better;
In good turns they woont be debtor.
An so comely,
An' so hwomely,
Be the maidens, if your son
Took oone o'm, then you'd cry 'Well done!
Friend an' wife,
Faethers, mothers, sisters, brothers,
Happy, happy, be their life!
Vor Do'set dear,
Then gi'e oone cheer;

D'ye hear? Oone cheer!

If you do zee our good men travel,
Down a-voot, or on their meares,
Along the winden leanes o' gravel,
To the markets or the feairs,
Though their hosses cwoats be ragged,
Though the men be muddy-lagged,
Be em roughish,
Be em gruffish,
They be sound, an' they will stand
By what is right wi' heart an' hand.
Friend an' wife,
Faethers, mothers, sisters, brothers,
Happy, happy, be their life!
Yor Do'set dear,
Then gi'e oone cheer;
D'ye hear? Oone cheer!

Hay-Meaken

Tis merry ov a zummer's day,
Where vo'k be out a-meaken hay;
Where men an' women, in a string,
Do ted or turn the grass, an' zing,
Wi' cheemen vaices, merry zongs,
A-tossen o' their sheenen prongs
Wi' earms a-zwangen left an' right,
In colour'd gowns an' shirtsleeves white;

Or, wider spread, a reaken round
The rwosy hedges o' the ground,
Where Sam do zee the speckled sneake,
An' try to kill en wi' his reake;
An' Poll do jump about an' squall,
To zee the twisten slooworm crawl.

Tis merry where a gay-tongued lot
Ov hay-meakers be all a-squot,
On lightly-russlen hay, a-spread
Below an elem's lofty head,
To rest their weary limbs an' munch
Their bit o' dinner, or their nunch;
Where teethy reakes do lie all round
By picks a-stuck up into ground.
An' wi' their vittles in their laps,
An' in their hornen cups their draps
O' cider sweet, or frothy eale,
Their tongues do run wi' joke an' teale.

An' when the zun, so low an' red,
Do sheen above the leafy head
O' zome broad tree, a-rizen high
Avore the vi'ry western sky,
Tis merry where all han's do goo
Athirt the groun', by two an' two,
A-reaken, over humps an' hollors,
The russlen grass up into rollers.

An' woone do row it into line,
An' woone do clwose it up behine;
An' after them the little bwoys
Do stride an' fling their earms all woys,
Wi' busy picks, an' proud young looks
A-mtciken up their tiny pooks.
An' zoo 'tis merry out among
The vo'k in hay-vield all day long.

Our Bethpleace

How dear's the door a latch do shut,
An' gearden that a hatch do shut,
'Where vu'st our bloomen cheaks ha' prest
The pillor ov our childhood's rest:
Or where, wi' little tooes, we wore
The paeths our faethers trod avore;
Or clim'd the timber's bark aloft,
Below the ziugen lark aloft,
The while we heard the echo sound
Droo all the ringen valley round.

A lwonesome grove o' woak did rise,
To screen our house, where smoke did rise,
A-twisten blue, while eet the zun
Did langthen on our childhood's fun;
An' there, wi' all the sheapes an' sounds
O' life, among the timber'd grounds,

The birds upon their boughs did zing,
An' milkmaids by their cows did zing,
Wi' merry sounds, that softly died,
A-ringen down the valley zide.

By river banks, wi' reeds a-bound,
An' sheenen pools, with weeds a-bound,
The long-neck'd gander's ruddy bill
To snow-white geese did cackle sh'ill;
An' striden peewits heasten'd by,
O' tiptooe wi' their screamen cry;
An' stalken cows a-lowen loud,
An' strutten cocks a-crowen loud,
Did rouse the echoes up to mock
Their mingled soun's by hill an' rock.

The stars that cliin'd our skies all dark,
Above our sleepen eyes all dark,
An' zuns a-rollen round to bring
The seasons on, vrom spring to spring,
Ha' vied, wi' never-resten flight,
Droo green-bough'd dae, an' dark-treed night;
Till now our childhood's pleaces there
Be gay wi' other feaces there,
An' we ourselves do vollow on
Our own forelivers dead an' gone.

Beach at Weymouth Past & Present Publications

BISHOP'S CAENDLE

At peace dae, who but we should goo
To Caendle vor an hour or two:
As gay a dae as ever broke
Above the heads o' Caendle vo'k,
Vor peace, a-come vor all, did come
To them wi' two new friends at hwome.
Zoo while we kept, wi' nimble peace,
The wold dun tow'r avore our feace,
The air at laste begun to come
Wi' drubbens ov a beaten drum;
An' then we heard the horns' loud droats
Play off a tuen's upper notes;
An' a'ter that a risen chearm
Vrom tongues o' people in a zwarm:
An' zoo, at laste, we stood among
The merry feaces o' the drong.

An' there we vound, wi' garlands tied
In wreaths an bows on every zide,
An' color'd flags, a-flutt'ren high
An' bright avore the sheenen sky,
The very d'rection-post a-drest
Wi' posies on his earms an' breast.
At laste, the vo'k zwarm'd in by scores
An' hundreds droo the gert barn doors,

To dine on English feare in ranks
A-zot on chairs, or stools, or planks,
By teables reachen row an' row,
Wi' cloths as white as driven snow.
An' while they took, wi' merry cheer,
Ther pleaces at the meat an' beer,
The band did blow an' beat aloud
Ther merry tuens to the crowd;
An' slowly-zwiugen flags did spread
Ther hangen colors auver head.
An' then the vo'k wi' jay an' pride,
Stood up in stillness, zide by zide,
Wi' downcast heads, the while ther friend
Rose up avore the teable's end,
An' zaed a timely greace, an' blest
The welcome meat to every guest.
An' then a-rose a mingled naise
O' knives an' pleates, an' cups an' trays.

An' tongues wi merry tongues a-drowned
Below a deaf nen storm o' sound.
An' zoo, at laste, their worthy host
Stood up to gie 'em all a twoast,
That they did drink, wi' shouts o' glee,
An' whirlen earms to dree times dree.
An' when the bwoards at laste wer beare

Ov' all the cloths an' goodly feare,
An' froth noo longer rose to zwim
'Ithin the beermug's sheenen rim,
The vo'k, a-streamen droo the door,
Went out to geames they had in store.
An' on the blue-reav'd waggon's bed,
Above his vower wheels o' red,
Musicians zot in rows, and play'd
Ther tuens up to chap an' maid,
That beat, wi' playsome tooes an' heels,
The level ground in nimble reels.
An' zome agean, a-zet in line,
An' starten at a given sign,
Wi' outreach'd breast, a-breathen quick
Droo op'nen lips, did nearly kick
Ther polls, a-runnen sich a peace,
Wi' streamen heair, to win the reace.
An' in the house, an' on the green,
An' in the shrubb'ry's leafy screen,
On ev'ry zide we zeed sich lots
O' smilen frieuds in happy knots,
That I do think, that droo the feast
In Caendle, vor a dae at least,
You woudden vind a scowlen feace
Or dumpy heart in all the pleace.

MY ORCHET IN LINDEN LEA

Ithin the woodlands, flow'ry gleaded,
By the woak tree's mossy moot,
The sheenen grass-bleades, timber-sheaded,
Now do quiver under voot;
An' birds do whissle auver head,
An' water's bubblen in its bed,
An' there vor me the apple tree
Do lean down low in Linden Lea.

When leaves that leately wer a-springen
Now do feade 'ithin the copse,
An' painted birds do hush ther zingen
Up upon the timber's tops ;
An' brown-leav'd fruit's a-turnen red,
In cloudless zunsheen, auver head,
Wi' fruit vor me, the apple tree
Do lean down low in Linden Lea.

Let other vo'k meake money vaster
In the air o' dark-room'd towns,
I don't dread a peevish measter;
Though noo man do heed my frowns,
I be free to goo abrode,
Or teake agean my hwomeward road
To where, vor me, the apple tree
Do lean down low in Linden Lea.

43

'An Olde Dorset Songster'

If you had happened to be walking through Sturminster Newton in Dorset about a hundred years ago, you might have seen a bearded man being pushed around in a basket chair. This would probably have been ROBERT YOUNG, or as his alter ago was called, RABIN HILL. Less well known than WILLIAM BARNES, Robert Young was an interesting character who played his part in capturing the Dorset dialect in writing. While Barnes's poems were of a more serious, thoughtful nature, Hill's speciality was comic poetry. Perhaps it was his background as a tailor which gave him an insight into the peculiarities of human nature.

It is thought that the coming of the railways inspired Young to start writing. He said: 'About the time that the Somerset and Dorset line … was opened [1861] some very amusing incidents occurred that induced me to record them in verse in the dialect.' A great deal of the comedy was derived from the reception that the railways received from the local people. It was for this that Young first created the character of an old farm worker called 'Rabin Hill', who was bewildered by the railways, in poems such as 'Rabin Hill's Visit to the Railway; What he Zeed and Done and What he Zed About It'. This was followed by 'Rabin Hill's Excursion to Weston-Super-Mare to see the Opening of the New Pier'. Robert Young's friends encouraged them to print his poems privately and his writing career soon took off. But it was his recollections of his life, written down painstakingly in an exercise book, which also helped to keep alive the realities and the voices of the past. These have been reinvigorated by Dr Alan Chedzoy of Weymouth in a new edition of Robert Young's Early Years, published by the Dorset Record Society.

The isolation of Dorset, which has been before spoken of, has had much to do with preserving from extinction the old dialect spoken in the days of the Wessex kings. Within its boundaries, especially in 'outstep placen', as the people call them, the old speech may be heard in comparative purity. Let it not be supposed that Dorset is an illiterate corruption of literary English. It is an older form of English; it possesses many words that elsewhere have become obsolete, and a grammar with rules as precise as those of any recognised language. No one not to the manner born can successfully imitate the speech of the rustics who, from father to son, through many generations have lived in the same village. A stranger may pick up a few Dorset words, only, in all probability, to use them incorrectly. For instance, he may hear the expression 'thic tree' for 'that tree', and go away with the idea that 'thic' is the Dorset equivalent of 'that', and so say 'thic grass' – an expression which no true son of the Dorset soil would use; for, as the late

*William Barnes pointed out, things in Dorset are of two classes :
(i) The personal class of formed things, as a man, a tree, a boot;
(2) the impersonal class of unformed quantities of things, as a
quantity of hair, or wood, or water. 'He' is the personal pronoun for
class (1); 'it' for class (2).*

*Similarly, 'thease' and 'thic' are the demonstratives of class (1);
'this' and 'that' of class (2). A book is 'he'; some water is 'it'. We
say in Dorset: 'Thease tree by this water', 'Thic cow in that grass'.
Again, a curious distinction is made in the infinitive mood: when
it is not followed by an object, it ends in 'y'; when an object follows,
the 'y' is omitted: 'Can you mowy?' but 'Can you mow this grass
for me?' The common use of 'do' and 'did' as auxiliary verbs, and
not only when emphasis is intended, is noteworthy (the 'o' of the
'do' being faintly heard). 'How do you manage about threading
your needles?' asked a lady of an old woman engaged in sewing,
whose sight was very dim from cataract. The answer came: 'Oh, he
[her husband] do dread 'em for me.' In Dorset we say not only 'today' and 'to-morrow', but also 'to-week', 'to-year'. 'Tar'ble' is often
used for 'very', in a good as well as a bad sense. There are many
words bearing no resemblance to English in Dorset speech. What
modern Englishman would recognise a 'mole hill' in a 'wont-
heave', or 'cantankerous' in 'thirtover'?*

*But too much space would be occupied were this fascinating subject
to be pursued further. National schools, however, are corrupting*

Wessex speech, and the niceties of Wessex grammar are often neglected by the children. Probably the true Dorset will soon be a thing of the past. William Barnes' poems and Thomas Hardy's Wessex novels, especially the latter, will then become invaluable to the philologist. In some instances Mr Barnes' spelling seems hardly to represent the sound of words as they are uttered by Dorset, or, as they say here, 'Darset' lips.

From *Memorials of old Dorset* by THOMAS PERKINS, *published 1907*

Bridport East St. Past & Present Publications

Listen to Dorset's past

It's one thing to read Dorset dialect on the page, but another to hear it. You can now listen to old Dorset dialect for yourself, thanks to the fascinating online Sounds collection from the British Library. Go to **http://sounds.bl.uk** to find out more. In the *Nick and Mally Dow English Folk Music collection*, you can listen to songs like *'The man who uses the brush'*, performed by NORMAN HOUSE in Beaminster in 1984, and *'You'll want me back some day'*, performed by retired hurdle maker and thatcher, BILL HOUSE in Beaminster in 1986. You can also hear recordings of conversations with Dorset people about accent, dialect and attitudes to language. One of these is a conversation in Portesham with SID HODDER, a retired farm worker born in 1878. Sid talks about traditional stacking and threshing techniques. In another recording, JOHN SYMONDS, a retired farmer born in 1871, looks back at the wages he earned when he first started work and talks about the amount of cider drunk by farm workers!

Thomas Hardy and Wessex

No exploration of the writers of Dorset would be complete without a look at THOMAS HARDY and 'Wessex', as he referred to his fictional world in the south and south-west

Thomas Hardy Creative Commons

of England. Hardy's novels are set in the world of Dorset, and Dorset's landscape and history is now full of associations with Hardy. Hardy was tutored by WILLIAM BARNES and greatly influenced by him. He was also part of an unusual literary meeting which took place in Dorset at The King's Head Hotel in Dorchester. It seems that ROBERT LOUIS STEVENSON was taking a trip from Bournemouth to Exmoor to help improve his health. On the way, he stopped in Dorchester and met with Hardy. Hardy was still to publish *Tess of the d'Urbervilles* (in 1891), which Stevenson found a little too risqué for his taste. The two writers were never to meet again.

Hardy's Dorset

You could say that Dorset forms an additional character in many of Hardy's novels. Here are just a few of those settings:

Dorchester (Casterbridge)
Dorset's county town plays a major role in Hardy country, not least for its place as the setting, under the name of Casterbridge, of the novel *The Mayor of Casterbridge*.

Shaftesbury
Every Hardy fan will recognise Shaftesbury. This is because it has an essential part to play in the unfolding of events in both *Jude the Obscure* and *Tess of the d'Urbervilles*.

Egdon Heath

Egdon Heath is an atmospheric force in Hardy's novels and is thought to be Hardy's name for a number of individual heaths near Dorchester. Egdon Heath plays a key part in *The Return of the Native* and also features in *The Mayor of Casterbridge*. The heath has shrunk in size since it was first explored by a young Hardy, but there has been good news in more recent times. In November 2014, the National Trust acquired 200-acre Slepe Heath, part of the heathland believed to make up Egdon Heath, for £650,000. As well as helping to preserve an important part of Dorset's cultural landscape, this should also help to protect rare flora and fauna on the heath.

Puddletown (Weatherbury)
Back to the Piddles and Puddles again! Hardy's family history was closely bound up with Puddletown. His grandfather and great-grandfather were Puddletown natives, so it's no wonder that the place, as Weatherbury, was featured in *Under the Greenwood Tree* and *Far From the Madding Crowd*.

The home of Dorset's literary greats
If you're planning a visit to Dorset and looking to explore the county's literary history, a great place to start is the Dorset County Museum in Dorchester. Not only does the museum host a complete replica of Thomas Hardy's study at his house, Max Gate, it is also home to many books and other mementoes of his past. As well as gaining a fascinating insight into Hardy, you can also discover books and papers on WILLIAM BARNES and ROBERT YOUNG. You can discover more about the museum at: **www.dorsetcountymuseum. org/writers_dorset**

Dorset: a world of inspiring words

The Durdle Door iStock

Dorset has been home – and host – to many other writers besides its most famous characters. For some, it provided a lifetime's inspiration, while for others the county played a brief, though memorable, part.

Dorset's dramatic Isle of Purbeck was the inspiration behind ENID BLYTON'S adventure stories for children. Following Blyton's first visit to the area in the 1930s, it became an evocative setting in her books, with specific landmarks making an appearance. It's not only Dorset's landscape which helped to shape Blyton's books. The writer bought Purbeck Golf Club for £1 and she used to take holidays in Swanage. It is said that the character of *Mr Plod the policeman* from her *Noddy* books is based on a real one, a Studland policeman of those days, possibly PC CHRISTOPHER RHONE!

Fossil on the Jurassic coast - Lyme-Regis iStock

Weymouth Sea Front Past & Present Publications

Bath may be the place with which JANE AUSTEN is most associated, but Dorset also played a part in her work. The author regularly visited Lyme Regis and it was there that she wrote *Persuasion*. Lyme Regis is also where JOHN FOWLES set his classic novel *The French Lieutenant's Woman*.

Of the prolific Powys family, it is the Powys brothers who seemed to be most influenced by Dorset in their works.

You'll find the county featured in the books of JOHN COWPER POWYS, T.F. POWYS and LLEWELYN POWYS. John was the author of a number of Wessex-based novels, including *Weymouth Sands* and *Maiden Castle*. His brother T.F. POWYS wrote novels and short stories which made Dorset their setting, but it is LLEWELYN POWYS's Dorset essays which are seen to be among the greatest ever written about the county.

Dorset's Chesil Beach was the setting for JOHN MEADE FALKNER's novel about Dorset smugglers, Moonfleet. In fact, Falkner used a great deal of the county as a setting. For example, the headland in the book called *'The Snout'* is Portland Bill and the village of Moonfleet itself is based on East Fleet. Chesil Beach was also the eponymous setting for IAN MCEWAN's *On Chesil Beach*.

Dorset's influence on writers continues to this day. Writer CHRIS CHIBNALL (*Law and Order: UK, Doctor Who, Broadchurch*) lives on the Jurassic Coast and has found inspiration from the area. Dorset-based crime writer MINETTE WALTERS has used Dorset locations in many of her novels, such as *The Shape of Snakes*.

Today, Dorset is home to writers such as children's writer and illustrator BABETTE COLE and RACHEL BILLINGTON. The world of *Downton Abbey*, which has captivated so many people, was the creation of Dorset resident JULIAN FELLOWES, who first became internationally famous when his *Gosford Park* screenplay won an Oscar.

An offshore perspective on Portland iStock

There's something 'bunny' in Portland

In 2005, a wordy Dorset superstition meant a change had to be made to posters for a new Wallace and Gromit film! If you're a resident of Portland in Dorset, it's very likely that you will do anything to avoid saying the word 'rabbit'! As with many superstitions, this one has a kernel of truth. The old fear of rabbits was based on the fact that quarry men would often see rabbits emerging from their burrows immediately before a rock fall. With these rock falls often injuring or killing quarry workers, it is no wonder that rabbits became associated with bad luck. As a result, Portland people will use alternative ways to refer to the creatures, such as *'furry things'* or *'underground mutton'*! But when a new Wallace and Gromit film, *The Curse of the Were-Rabbit*, came to town a few years ago, the posters had to be changed. There was no mention of the crucial word. Instead the posters stated mysteriously that *'Something bunny is going on'*!

Portland Past & Present Publications

Portland sailors were also superstitious about rabbits. If they happened to see one before setting off on a journey, they refused to set sail that day. While we're on the subject of Portland and words, you might be interested to hear about an unusual nickname earned by Portland people. They were once known for being highly skilled at slinging pebbles! It may seem surprising, but this was helpful for keeping invaders away. It's a talent which apparently inspired THOMAS HARDY's name for Portland: *'The Isle of Slingers'*!

Scrumpy and Western

Dorset's dialect and style has in part been captured and kept alive by the music genre of Scrumpy and Western. Scrumpy and Western is an affectionate term for music which hails from the West Country, bringing together comical folk songs which affectionately take the mickey out of modern songs while using the local dialect. Most people have heard of THE WURZELS from Somerset, who found fame thanks to their number one hit, *Combine Harvester*. Dorset's equivalent is the group THE YETTIES, who hail from Yetminster. If you're a fan of Radio 4, you'll know their music. It is their version of *Barwick Green* which has introduced the Sunday morning omnibus edition of *The Archers* for almost 40 years.

Sherborne Castle iStock

Despite all this THE YETTIES have never lost their genuine feeling for the countryside. They now live in Sherborne (just a few miles from Yetminster) and they draw on their personal experiences of country life for their concert programme. Some of the songs they sing recall what life was like when they were kids helping the farmers at harvest time, scrumping when the farmers weren't looking, raiding the hedges, fields and woods for food and eating rabbit for practically every meal. They talk of village characters and village occasions and create the atmosphere of the village social.

From www.theyetties.co.uk

THE YETTIES retired in 2011 and lead musician Pete Shutler sadly died in 2014.

Another Dorset folk group was WHO'S A'FEARD, who took their name from the motto on Dorset's crest. The group has now disbanded, but two members went on to form THE SKIMMITY HITCHERS. While it's important to acknowledge modern contributions to the Dorset folk scene, it is also interesting to note that THOMAS HARDY played a part in capturing local folk music. Hardy is famed for his Wessex novels, but people are less aware of his enduring love for Dorset folk songs and dances.

'The Piddles and the Puddles'

Poole Harbour iStock

You don't have to go far in Britain to realise that it's packed full of some wonderfully quirky place names. This seems particularly true of Dorset! One particularly endearing aspect of this is what are known locally as *'The Piddles and the Puddles'*! While this may sound like a reference to some kind of plumbing problem, it is in fact a poetic way of referring to local places! These are the wonderful old place names near to the *River Piddle* in Dorset. Just some of them are *Piddlehinton, Piddletrenthide, Tolpuddle* and *Puddletown!* The name actually comes from the Anglo-Saxon word *pidelle*, which means 'boggy or marshy ground'. Two of the areas that supply the initial water for the river are fittingly called *Soggy Wood* and *Rake's Bottom!*

So what happened to lead to the change of place names such as *Briantpuddle* and *Puddletown?* The popular myth is that the locals changed their village titles to avoid embarrassing QUEEN VICTORIA while she was visiting because it was felt that the original names were too vulgar! While this is a great story, there are some who say that this is inaccurate and suggest that it was actually to spare the blushes of the employees of the GPO's telegraph service! In 1956, Dorset County Council tried to change *Puddletown* to *Piddletown*, but residents objected! The *'piddle'* theme continues in strength in *Piddletrenthide*, where you can visit the *Piddle Inn*! *Piddlehinton* is the home of the *Dorset Piddle Brewery* which makes beers with names like *Piddle, Cocky* and *Slasher*!

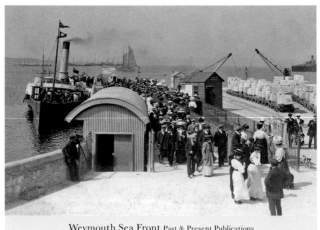

Weymouth Sea Front Past & Present Publications

Odd or unusual Dorset place names

There's even more to Dorset place names than *'the Piddles and the Puddles'!* While to a contemporary ear, some may sound a bit rude, they all have a little poetry about them!

BARBERS PILES, Poole

BELCHALWELL, near Sturminster Newton

CLAPGATE, near Wimborne

CRUMPET'S FARM DRIVE, Lytchett Matravers, Poole

DROOP, near Blandford Forum

DUNGY HEAD, near West Lulworth

GOATHORN CLOSE, Poole

HAPPY BOTTOM, near Corfe Mullen

KNOBCROOK ROAD, in Wimborne

PISTLE DOWN, near Verwood

PITT BOTTOM, Lytchett Matravers

SCRATCHY BOTTOM, Lulworth

SHAGGS, East Lulworth

SHAGGS MEADOW, Lyndhurst

SHATTERS HILL, Wareham

SHITTERTON, near Bere Regis

There's no getting away from the rudeness of this place-name, though it's actually derived from the meaning for 'a farm on a stream which is used as a sewer'! It is frequently listed on lists of the world's rudest place names! In fact, in 2012, Shitterton was voted 'Britain's worst place name' in a survey carried out by genealogy website *Find my Past*. Shitterton has frequently had its village sign stolen by tourists who appreciate the name just a little too much. This was why, in 2010, the inhabitants got together to purchase a 1.5-ton block of Purbeck Stone to place at the entrance to Shitterton, carved with the hamlet's name! It's good to hear that, despite the prudish Victorians once changing the name to Sitterton, the place reverted back to its original name!

SLOP BOG, nature reserve in Ferndown

TINCLETON, near Dorchester

A Telegram to the King

The Society of Dorset Men was set up to provide support, connections and an opportunity to celebrate all things Dorset. It is thought that there were friendly meetings of Dorset men working in London as far back as the 17th century. Each year, in advance of the annual dinner of the Society of Dorset Men, they sent the current King or Queen a telegram, in dialect. In 1950, the telegram said:

To His Majesty King Jarge,

Oonce more, the Zociety o' Darset Men, voregather'd round their vestive bwoard at th' Darchester Hotel vor their Yearly Junket, d' zend Yer Most Graishus Majesty their dootiful greetins and expression of unswerven loyalty an' devotion. May Yer Majesty be zpared to us vor many years as our pattern an' guide.

I d' bide, vor all time,

Yer Vaithful Zarvint and Counsellor

West Bay Bridport Past & Present Publications

Dorset dishes

Read on to discover some of the dishes and delicacies for which Dorset is known!

Rook Pie

It may sound an unlikely dish to us now, but rook pie was once a popular and affordable meal for labourers in Dorset and elsewhere.

Lettuce Soup

Light, refreshing lettuce soup was once a traditional favourite in Dorset. Not only did it taste delicious, it also made the most of the many lettuces available in the area during the summer!

Piddle Bacon Cake

This was an old delicacy which once underwent a change of name. The Victorians were not impressed by the fact that the dish was named after the River Piddle because they thought that the place name was rather offensive! The dish was renamed Puddle Bacon Cake, but has now regained its much more characterful original name!

Cabbages

Did you know that Dorset was the first county in England

to cultivate cabbages? Sir Anthony Ashley of Wimborne St Giles introduced the vegetable from Holland to his estate! If you take a look at Sir Anthony's effigy in the village church, you'll notice a vegetable at his feet which closely resembles a cabbage...

iStock

Dorset Apple Cake

As the name would suggest, Dorset Apple Cake is the region's answer to the popular treat, apple cake. The county's version combines the fruit with spices and the option of nuts like almonds and walnuts. Apple Cake is highly popular right now, thanks to the influence of The Great British Bake-Off, but if you want to go traditional, you'll need to make sure that you use the 'rubbed-in' method mixed with milk to give a more scone-like mixture!

Dorset Cream Teas

Cornwall and Devon may be famed for their cream teas, but the Dorset equivalent is not far behind! Just imagine looking at the view over the lovely Dorset countryside, enjoying home-made scones with clotted cream and jam or perhaps a slice or two of Dorset Apple Cake along with some freshly made tea. *Delicious!*

iStock

Frumenty

Popular at fairs in many parts of Europe, this ancient dish was also popular in Dorset. Frumenty was once an important part of the traditional Celtic Christmas meal. Frumenty with rum (or *'Furmity'*) played a crucial role in the downfall of Thomas Hardy's Mayor of Casterbridge. Frumenty often consisted of boiled or cracked wheat. The recipes vary, but some feature broth, while others add eggs or milk. There were sweeter versions which included almonds, currants and other ingredients.

Dorset Blue Vinny

Another food which takes its name and heritage from Dorset is Dorset Blue Vinny (or Vinney). Said to go very well with Dorset Knobs, Blue Vinny is firm white cheese made from partially skimmed cow's milk. While some believe that the cheese takes the 'vinny' part of its name from the Old English word for mould, fyne, others think that 'vinney' comes from a Dorset phrase linked to a now defunct word vinew which means 'to become mouldy'. There are others who think that the word 'vinny' comes from the word 'veiny' as a description of the distinctive blue veins marking the cheese! It is said that, many years ago, the mould was grown by placing old shoes or harnesses in milk! No wonder the cheese-makers' locations were kept secret for fear of closure. One slightly less plausible tale about Blue Vinny was that a train once ran on old cheeses in the place of wheels, thanks to the toughness of its rind! There even used to be whispers that Blue Vinny was available on the black market many years ago... While Blue Vinny almost became a thing of the past, it has now made a comeback. Nowadays it is made commercially and available to enjoy with a Dorset Knob or two!

Woont ye have brown bread a-put ye,
An' some vinny cheese a-cut ye?
From 'Praise O' Dorset', by William Barnes

Dorset Knobs

Dorset Knobs are savoury biscuits said to take their strange name from their resemblance to Dorset Knob buttons or actual door knobs! Crafted from bread dough packed with extra helpings of sugar and butter, Dorset Knobs are light, crisp and crumbly to eat and go well dipped in tea or enjoyed with a wedge of Blue Vinny cheese. They were even said to be a favourite of Thomas Hardy! Once made by a number of companies, Dorset Knobs are now made by just one company, Moore Biscuits. Dorset Knobs are special for yet another reason. They're only made during January and February each year!

How many biscuits are celebrated with their own festival?

The Dorset Knob is the star attraction in a special event that takes place in the Dorset village of Cattistock each year on the first Sunday in May. In the **Dorset Knob Throwing and Food Festival event**, participants have to attempt to hurl a Dorset Knob as far as they can! But that's not all. Visitors can also enjoy the delights of events such as knob eating, a knob and spoon race, knob darts, knob painting and guess the weight of the knob. So far no one has beaten the current record throw of 29.4 metres (96 feet) which was achieved in 2012!

THE RULES FOR DORSET KNOB THROWING

1. Three Dorset Knobs per go, furthest knob thrown is measured.
2. Use only Dorset Knobs provided.
3. Standing throw from marked standing point.
4. Underarm throwing only.
5. One foot must remain on the ground during throwing.
6. Distance of the furthest knob only measured within the designated throwing zone, which is 5 metres wide x 32 metres long, marked in 2-metre zones, with use of measure in-between marks to determine distance thrown.
7. Dorset Knob measured at final resting place.
8. If Dorset Knob breaks upon landing it will be the umpire's decision of final resting place.

From www.dorsetknobthrowing.com

A few words about breakfast

Dewbit – the first meal in the morning, not so substantial as a regular breakfast. The agricultural labourers in some parts of Dorsetshire were accustomed some years since to say that in harvest time they required seven meals in the day: dewbit, breakfast, nuncheon, cruncheon, nammit, crammit, and supper. But this seems to have been rather a quaint jingle than an enumeration of meals, as some of them, nuncheon and nammit, for example, clearly indicate the same.

From *Glossary of Dorset Dialect*, by WILLIAM BARNES, *published 1863*

Dorset: did you know?

One of the world's most popular board games first had its start in Dorset! This is because many of the questions for the original version of *Trivial Pursuit* were researched in the public library in Weymouth!

Dorset is thought to be where the **Black Death** (or the Great Pestilence or Great Mortality as it was known by people at that time) first came to Britain. It is believed that two ships docking at Weymouth in June 1348 brought the deadly disease to the country. Melcombe, close to Weymouth, was the first place in which the epidemic began, from a sailor who had been to Gascony. The Black Death eventually died down, but not before around half of the country's population had died of the disease.

Britain's first **fossil shop** was opened in Lyme Regis in 1826! It was run by MARY ANNING and her family, who survived by digging fossils from the cliffs to sell to holidaymakers. Mary went on to become a recognised expert in the field and was consulted by academics and even visited by KING FREDERICK AUGUSTUS II OF SAXONY.

Misty winter morning at Chalmouth Beach, Dorset, along the Jurassic Coast with people fossil hunting iStock

Gold Hill, Shaftesbury

Dorset's **Poole Harbour** is the largest natural harbour in Britain and said to be the second largest natural harbour in the world after Sydney! The harbour's Brownsea Island nature reserve was where Scouting first began, started by LORD BADEN-POWELL in 1907.

Dorset's distinctive **Portland Stone** is famous throughout the world. But did you know that this pale limestone from the Jurassic period was used to create St Paul's Cathedral, Buckingham Palace and the Cenotaph? Portland Stone was also used to make all the First and Second World War soldiers' gravestones. It is also featured in high-profile buildings throughout the world.

Did you know that what is seen by many as **the world's earliest radio station** was set up by MARCONI at the Haven Hotel, Sandbanks in Poole? MARCONI built a transmitter there in 1899!

You'll probably recognise **Gold Hill** in Shaftesbury thanks to a very famous advert for bread! The hill was immortalised by an advert for Hovis bread which showed a delivery boy pushing a bike up the picturesque street.

It may sound surprising, but a **chilli pepper** grown in Dorset is claimed to be the **world's hottest!** If you have to handle the **Dorset Naga**, you'll need gloves to protect yourself!

The oldest farmed herd in the country is believed to be the one at Abbotsbury in Dorset – a herd of swans! Records shows that a swannery was based in Abbotsbury as far back as 1393. Today the swannery is the world's only managed colony of nesting swans and the only place in the world where you can walk through the heart of a colony of nesting mute swans. Visitors can help to handfeed 600 swans at feeding time at certain times of the year.

The swannery at Abbotsbury iStock

The Celtic name for Dorset, **'Dorseteschire'**, means *'the place of fisticuffs'!*

Dorset is part of the **Dorset and East Devon World Heritage Site** *(the Jurassic Coast):* this is the only natural world heritage site on the UK mainland and spans almost the entire length of Dorset's coast.

Dorset is the birthplace of the trade union movement! This was thanks to the Tolpuddle Martyrs, farm labourers who set up a union in Tolpuddle in 1834 to give them more power to tackle their impoverished conditions. However, despite the fact that unions were lawful, six of the union's leaders were arrested and sentenced to seven years' transportation for taking an oath of secrecy. This injustice led to a huge public protest throughout the country with thousands of people marching through London and many petitions and protest meetings. The fightback worked and the martyrs were brought back to Dorset! The martyrs and the power of solidarity are commemorated each summer with a festival on Tolpuddle's Village Green. The event draws dedicated trade unionists from around the globe.

Sources

www.theguardian.com/commentisfree/2012/jan/24/
william-barnes-england-robbie-burns

https://archive.org/index.php

www.bournemouthecho.co.uk/news/11058774.21_of_the_
funniest_place_names_in_Dorset_and_the_New_Forest/

http://news.bbc.co.uk/local/dorset/hi/people_and_places/
arts_and_culture/newsid_8158000/8158886.stm

http://realwestdorset.co.uk/2011/05/queen-victoria-dorset-
piddle-villages-name-changes/

www.pri.org/stories/2013-08-19/piddle-or-puddle-curious-
little-english-river

http://old.qi.com/talk/viewtopic?t=1837&start=0&sid
=6344de193278682cacd54f22e3

www.funtrivia.com/playquiz/quiz35795128fa290.html

http://news.bbc.co.uk/1/hi/england/dorset/4318710.stm

www.dorsetcountymuseum.org/writers_dorset

www.thewordtravels.com/thomas-hardy-and-dorset.html

www.britainexpress.com/History/bio/hardy-tours.htm

http://commons.wikimedia.org/wiki/File:Wessex.png

http://realwestdorset.co.uk/2010/09/british-library-reveals-
dorset-songs-stories-map-archival-sound-recordings/

http://news.bbc.co.uk/local/dorset/hi/people_and_places/
history/newsid_8664000/8664479.stm

www.theyetties.co.uk/history.

Available now

Black Country Dialect
Bristol Dialect
Cockney Dialect
Cornish Dialect
Derbyshire Dialect
Devon Dialect
Essex Dialect
Glaswegian Dialect
Hampshire Dialect
Kentish Dialect
Lancashire Dialect
Liverpool Dialect
Manchester Dialect
Newcastle Dialect
Norfolk Dialect
Somerset Dialect
Suffolk Dialect
Sussex Dialect
Warwickshire Dialect
Yorkshire Dialect

Available in 2015

Evolving English Word Bank
Lincolnshire Dialect
Nottinghamshire Dialect
Scottish Dialects
The Cotswolds Dialect
The Lake District Dialect
Wiltshire Dialect
Leicestershire Dialect

See website for more details. Bradwellbooks.com